*It's spiritual,
practical,
and inspirational*

Copyright © 2021 by Claudia Thompson

All rights reserved. No part of this publication may be reproduced, distributed, or transmitted in any form or by any means, including photocopying, recording, or other electronic or mechanical methods, without the prior written permission of the publisher, except in the case of brief quotations embodied in critical reviews and certain other noncommercial uses permitted by copyright law. For permission requests, write to the publisher, addressed "Attention: Permissions Coordinator," at the address below.

Alpha Book Publisher
727 main st,
Moosic, PA 18507
www.alphapublisher.com

Ordering Information:
Quantity sales. Special discounts are available on quantity purchases by corporations, associations, and others. For details, contact the publisher at the address above. Orders by U.S. trade bookstores and wholesalers. Visit
www.alphapublisher.com/contact-us to learn more.

Printed in the United States of America

Waiting on Our Own Weights
Claudia E.C. Thompson

Dedication

This book is dedicated in the memory of my mother, Martina R. Bryant Carruth, a woman with great principles and strength. She always encouraged me to write and use the God given talent granted to me. My mother taught us to go after our goals in life, and she was our greatest supporter in doing it. She never held a grudge and always taught her children to get along and be independent. She was a woman of great vitality, and her teachings are forever in my heart and spirit. She illustrated strength in the eyes of her children, and even when life became challenging, her strength soared above it all. The time and effort dedicated to this manuscript is from the prayers and faithfulness of my mother's investment in me.

Table of Contents

Introduction 9

Chapter 1: Discovery 12

Chapter 2: Break the Cycle 18

Chapter 3: If Not Now, When 25

Chapter 4: Focus 35

Chapter 5: Move 41

Chapter 6: Pick Up the Pace 48

Chapter 7: Plan to Win 54

Chapter 8: Mine Your Own Business 60

Chapter 9: Pay Attention 65

Chapter 10: Don't Judge the View 70

Chapter 11: Fight 73

Chapter 12: Health Weights 77

Chapter 13: Live 82

Chapter 14: Gratitude 87

Chapter 15: The Best of You 92

Introduction

When thinking of the challenges and detainments of our life, usually we do not initially think that the delay may be caused by ourselves. Our first thought is to believe that those things around us, or associated with us, are the factors that could result in the hurdles we acquire. It is human nature to always believe that we are doing the very best that we can from day to day, however, to unfold the process of evaluating ourselves, as the possible obstruction to our own advancement, may possibly shatter our ego. It is a process within itself to start making an assessment of who we really are, beginning with the judgment of our own mind and pathway of our thoughts. Rarely do we associate the weights of our existence originating from the person within. However, broadening our perspective onto other people, or things, that are in our environment and community, without reversing the spotlight upon ourselves first, is almost always an impediment within itself.

Why does our curiosity seem to coerce us to the measure that we neglect the soul in which we occupy? Often our response is that other people and things are more captivating, or better yet, they are entertaining. Anything to divert the spotlight elsewhere. Regardless of our ethnicity, hereditary history, or economic framework, beginning the process of overcoming malfunctions that may occupy our internal space may be something to be reckoned with.

So who will we point the finger at, when the bumps in the road of life cause the route in which we travel to become too difficult to ride upon? And who then owns the responsibility to the winding curves that the path now presents? Evaluations require the action of making assessments, taking in considerations, estimations, and judgments of the matters present. Such evaluations often produce a pause in time, an opinion, and thought, into the existing focal point. Therefore, how do we navigate our way forward when the outcome of our assessment pilots its way to the contender instead of the one and only you?

When the expectations and waiting become personal weights, how do we master the art of liberating the person within? No one ever wants to take ownership, that the appetite for their expectations, can turn into pressure, poundage, substance, influence, stress, power, or even a load to coexist with. As a born-again believer, the Bible instructs us to cast every care upon Him (The Lord Jesus) because he cares (1Peter 5:7). In addition, the Bible informs us of those that wait upon the Lord shall be renewed in their strength (Isa 40:31). However, how do we consider this to be an effective force, directly in the processing, of the person within?

Discovery

Chapter One

Having a sense of self-consciousness is one of the first steps in the identification of who we are and learning ourselves. The reveal of our motives, intentions, moods, temperament, desires, needs and fulfillments are definitely something to be reckoned with. During the development of our life journey, we are confident there is a familiarity with who we really are inwardly, surprisingly, when there is a life event or crisis that emerges, and "wow" then we are introduced to different emotions, thoughts and feelings, that have never surfaced, and must now be dealt with. There is a phrase that is often used, "Let's just sweep it under the rug," meaning hide it for now and just maybe it will be forgotten. However, making transactions with feelings and emotions? "Not" so fast. Out of sight is certainly not out of mind. We can be completely honest with ourselves, and begin the process of moving beyond the circumstances that have a current affect, or we can rationalize our way out of it by providing a justifiable answer that can only be validated internally. The outcome of self-vindication will only yield delay, frustration, and repetition. There is one person that knows all truths of who we are internally, and that is no other than God Himself. He is the creator of all things in heaven and the earth, the visible and the invisible, therefore He knows us the best.

Nevertheless, the responsibility to conqueror the skill of comprehending who we are, and gaining the mastery of allowing the process of life to yield its intended purpose, is an individual account. Once we are willing to be forthright, direct, truthful, candid, sincere, and straight with ourselves, then true discovery will birth, and life can begin to happen. Is help warranted and imperative? Most certainly, YES! We can do nothing of ourselves, the Bible states:

Chapter One: Discovery

Not that we are sufficient of ourselves to think of anything as coming from ourselves, but our sufficiency is from God (2 Corth.3:5). Can we confess things to each other? Most certainly. God created people for people, however, the proposition of obtaining help for delicate situations from another must be carefully evaluated. That individual must be non-judgmental, forgiving, honest, wise, have a panorama view, prayer oriented, and the ability to avoid their personal opinions unless invited to do so.

Discovering who we are, as the beautiful creatures that God has created, is truly a process that is often taken for granted or assumed to naturally exist. True discovery of knowing who we are inside and out is certainly more than just verbally declaring it to be so, though that is a step in the right direction. However, it is to have the ability to see yourself, know yourself, be 100% honest with yourself, and finally, be willing to help yourself by making the necessary

Chapter One: Discovery

adjustments it takes to make your life exactly what God proposed it to be. As humans, we are designed to be productive and fruitful because we all are given and provided with a gift of life to be utilized to benefit or bless others, whether it is the gift of giving, music, speaking, etc. or just using the uniqueness of your existence. The gifts are endless that God has placed in humanity. Nevertheless, it is our individual responsibility to tap into those gifts and find our place in the world with them. We are brilliant human beings that are larger than we seem to be aware of. Introduction into that part of our entity seems to be the challenge in which the struggle lies.

Therefore, once we are acquainted with the substance of what we are truly made of on the inside, we can then advance inwardly. Yes, advancement within must take it's posture first, and anchor itself before we can externally become effective, fruitful, and powerful to others. Advancement, internally, is the progress we have made, from making the necessary adjustments to ourselves, that aborts the repetition of failure, disappointment, stagnation, frustration, and fruitlessness. It is always God's will as individuals to prosper. The Bible expresses that the word of God will never return to Him unfilled but will always accomplish that which He pleases and prosper where He sends it (Isa.55:11). If we find ourselves repeating the same intentions from year to year without an outcome of accomplishment, then it is imperative that a good and honest look internally, must be without hesitation, and the next immediate course of action taken.

The goal is to overcome ourselves so that we can present our frailties, unbiased, approachable, wisdom filled, loving, forgiving and even-spirited, individuals to others. These distinctive characteristics are not necessarily easy to constrain, nevertheless, they are essential for being effective and prosperous. We are not by any means perfect individuals, and will always

Chapter One: Discovery

be striving toward self-improvement, therefore, it is paramount that we become and remain authentic within and to God our creator, while keeping that motto at the forefront of our mind. Our prayer must be, Lord grant me the strength and consistency to avoid giving myself justified causes, that will result in a pattern of unfulfilled desires, and deprivation of your purpose, being satisfied in my life.

Break the Cycle

Chapter Two

Usually when speaking of an interruption of anything, it often signifies an unwelcome or unwanted disturbance which has infringed upon something that has us on a particular momentum, that's preferred not to be broken. A cycle of any kind can be unpleasant and uncomfortable, or it may be very pleasurable, with a never-ending desire. The breaking of a cycle is deemed to yield pleasure, success, wholeness, and possibly be that which has originated from an welcomed source. Most of us would like to keep a good thing going and not become a bystander to witness it's termination. The pattern of winning, living large, and having most of the things in this life that we define as an accomplishment would be the achievement of a goal for almost anyone.

Furthermore, we must admit that the everyday routine and traditional ways that

Chapter Two: Break the Cycle

we live, as each individual knows it to be, can become unconsciously, a replicated daily way of performance in various areas of our life. Yes, that wonderful word "LIFE" is certainly a blessing in itself to have. The ability to awaken each day, consume food, and just breathe, is often not given a lot of thought, because it appears to just be very common and natural, to most individuals that have no economical or health disparities. Therefore, what are the consequences, when the unconscious routine that we have created for ourselves merges into a comfortable reprise that's so innocently, becomes a system that results in an unceasing carbon-copy of existence? Without even realizing, we are repeating the same thing annually that consequently yields the same outcome.

Looking and reaching, looking and reaching, looking and reaching, for that ultimate breakthrough that will change the course of our life, and that piece of the puzzle that will bring about, what we define as fulfillment.

Furthermore, have we ever stopped to think that just maybe, there is a part of that inner man that needs to be broken, and humbled before the big reveal? Jesus is a prime example of someone who follows God's plan for His life. "And being found in fashion as a man, he humbled himself, and became obedient unto death, even the death of the cross" (Phil 2:8). Therefore, if we are not learning from our experiences, and what we understand, is being contributed to the effort of living, then we must do a complete investigation and explore what and how we are representing life. One of the most challenging oppositions we face is the challenge of discipline and change.

Discipline and change completely withdraw us from our secured place of existence. It uncoils us from that safe zone. Who wants to feel uncomfortable or disentangled from what they are accustomed to on a norm? Who wants to squirm and agonize from a shift in position or that common place of

Chapter Two: Break the Cycle

performance? Not too many of us would volunteer for that committee. Well, that is the price, more times than not, to moving forward. If a person is not willing to be disciplined, then they are not willing to change or grow. A cycle is chaperoned by routine, patterns, and a rhythm. As long as the cycle is moving and not interrupted, all is well, however, disturb the rhythm, and it is likely to create a reaction of irritability, frustration, unwarranted accusations, and a faltering pathway. The process of progression is the order of movement that will require suspension of any monotonous functions. The majority of persons in this journey of life has an impulse of some type to an expectation. How to arrive, will determine the virtue of their desire.

The awakening of realizing that life has become a humdrum of predictable thinking, unchanged chitter-chatter, and self-regulating activities is an awe-inspiring eye opener. We are all provoked in life by something that will result in a shifting of

Chapter Two: Break the Cycle

position in our thinking, feeling, or performance. However, having the courage to take the leap that will yield a rupturing in what may be a relentless replica of daily existence, takes a spirit of hardihood. Cycle breaking is easier said than done. The performance of exiting from what have been months or years of the familiar, will thrust anyone into a new unspecified territory. Nevertheless, who said that breaking the sequence of a routine is so bad? A cycle will always repeat itself, with the inability to be the recipient of the innovative things. The biggest hindrance of the breaking of a cycle is FEAR. A word no one wants to own up to because most individuals see fear as just someone who is bashful of speaking in public, someone that is afraid of the dark, or afraid to drive a vehicle. Not so quick! Fear comes in many colors, shapes and sizes. It does not shy from heights, weights, color nor titles. When change is not an option of acceptance to examine, and excuses are being offered as to why change will not work, without the time allocated to examine

Chapter Two: Break the Cycle

its effects, it will unequivocally surrender FEAR.

Accomplished individuals that have reached their desired goals are those that have broken the routine of the familiar and launched into new territory, then shifted into a place of discovery. Yes, discovery of who they really are, and the strength and courage they possess. We say that God's word is true but fail to apply it to the core of our own shortcomings at the time of our struggles. The Bible states "I can do all things through Christ that strengthens me." (Phil 4:13) If this verse is permitted to marinate within our spirit, then the realization of knowing that nothing needs to be tackled solo, but it is all conquered with the help of God. It is always through His strength and power that victory in anything is won. Alone we falter every time, however, His unmerited favor (Grace) is always sufficient. The second biggest hindrance to cycle breaking is PEOPLE! The FEAR of what others will say, think, or feel toward us. The approval of what and

Chapter Two: Break the Cycle

how we move forward is all up to God. He is our judge, and help, as we allow our focus to be centered upon Him. What does that mean? Christ becomes our focal point. As our prayer will be to see things through His eyes, and our hearing listening for His voice. These ingredients will be our guide and destiny.

If Not Now, When?

Chapter Three

Procrastination is one of the most declining obstacles we are in conflict within the odyssey of life. It is debilitating, weakening, and an impairment that can become a chronic part of life that partners with us throughout time if it's not recognized for what it really is. We may find ourselves making excuses for our delay in the things we desire, need, or intend to do, nevertheless each time we exempt ourselves, from the behavior that must be modified to produce the necessary transition, it promotes a restriction that becomes an increasing pitfall. There is a phrase that states "time waits for no man." Yes, that most valued word is called TIME, and what does it exactly mean? Is it a moment, episode, experience, incident, a meter, measurement, case, point, an hour, minute, or second? What exactly is it? Or does it have a different meaning to each individual?

Chapter Three: If Not Now, When?

Well, it may be comforting to know that it is all of these components. We live and function in them all, one way or the other, however it is our mindset that determines how we comprehend them, and in what way each component will be utilized. There is one factor for certain, the past is gone, and no one can relive it, the future has not yet arrived, but we can look forward to it, therefore the NOW is the element we have to work with for sure. The Bible states "Today if ye will hear His voice, harden not your hearts" (Heb 4:7) In addition, the Bible also states, "Now is the accepted time; behold, now is the day of salvation." (2 Corth 6:2). It is a human weakness that we often pause, to the things we should now act upon however, but later ends in regret. The things we detain are innumerable, meanwhile, there is something about the present moment we shy away from, because it will hold us accountable to the release of something, that we are more, than likely uncomfortable with.

Chapter Three: If Not Now, When?

The Bible states, "Come now, you who say, Today or tomorrow we will go to such and such a city, spend a year there, buy and sell, and make a profit; whereas you do not know what *will happen* tomorrow. For what *is* your life? It is even a vapor that appears for a little time and then vanishes away. Instead, you *ought to* say, "If the Lord wills, we shall live and do this or that" (James 4:13-15 NKJV). The security that grows in our articulation of habitual procrastination attributes to insecurity, fear, and vulnerability. All what many of us repudiate admission to, nevertheless it prevails. No one needs to know but you and the Lord Jesus. Our inward struggles belong to no one, but in the heart of God. Therefore, what do we do with these many components that make up time? We can all attest to, that time does not stand still, but progress regardless of life's state of affairs. What does that say to us as humans, with a variety of idiosyncrasies? One major injunction is that we all have one chance at life, whether good, bad, or somewhere in between, just one shot at life and time is part of that factor. The more time we misuse, abuse or squander, it becomes our personal loss. There can be no finger pointing, casting of the blame game, or fault finding toward anyone, but as the figure of speech states "the proof is in the pudding."

Once we achieve taking the responsibility of our own impairment, the more readily we will become the individuals of purpose. Another figure of speech states "talk is cheap," meaning it is low in value without the action that follows. It also indicates there is often a price to be paid that accompanies the territory of commitment. Yes, it will take being committed to the art of acting now. Why, because it so frequently means change and transition on our part. If we are not willing to commit to change or transition, then we cannot be a beneficiary of growth. Our hands are always open and ready to receive from our God the things we most hope for, however, doing it in our time is usually the deal we choose to make. If we choose to pray about it first, it is certainly justifiable and the right thing to do. The Bible tells us; In all thy ways acknowledge Him, (the Lord) and He will direct our path (Proverbs 3:6). Therefore, when peace like a river attendeth our way, and God has sanctioned you for His purpose, then there is no reason for now to become later and from later to never, which all can be the sum of defeat. It is too often the story for many individuals in one manner or another.

The word "WHEN" indicates that it will be needed. Something that is expected to be at some point in time. Often a statement in question, waiting for an answer of some sort. The answer to when lies in each individual and no one can provide that answer but self, depending on the situation, the individual, the season, and many other things that may contribute to the arrival of the answer. It is understood, hopefully by most, that everything is not, as one would say "cut and dry" meaning without extenuating attachments. Nevertheless,

Chapter Three: If Not Now, When?

when it comes to the endeavor to move forward or just to move at all, we must emerge to make an appearance with ourselves about our position, and if this is where we will choose to suspend or retire the journey. How many times should the pattern be repeated? Even repeated designs in fabric have its parameters and are brought to the edge and tied off to conclude that course of fashion, and to move on to the next. The dilemma of making a decision that could significantly impact our life is not a decision to be made in haste, nevertheless, it cannot extend into eternity because father time will run its course.

It is not easy to turn the mirror on ourselves, even when we are certain that it is someone or something else that has caused or affected our deferment. It is understood that it exempts and liberates us from the demand to manage that cargo upon ourselves. However, the truth of the matter is that we are responsible for ourselves regardless of the surrounding factors. Yes, it is a painful realization that we can be our own force to fight against, nevertheless, it is a factuality that once acknowledged, as not only a possibility, but as an authentic way to see ourselves. There are only two individuals that we must face the truths regarding ourselves, and that is, ourselves and God. The truth about who we really are within, belongs internally for acknowledgement and confession.

Liberating with ourselves to make decisions to change will cause reset to occur, as expedient as our affirmation will develop within. The Bible states, Then Jesus said to those Jews who believed Him, "If you abide in My word, you are My disciples indeed. And you shall know the truth, and the truth shall make you free" (John 8:31-32). If the Son therefore shall make you free, ye shall be free indeed (8:36).

There is nothing like being unrestricted and at liberty for being available to allow the beauty of your inner spirit to be released. When there is a piece of ourselves constrained in any part of life, it suppresses our ability to make clear, honest, and forthright, decisions that we know are precipitated and inspired by the inspiration of the Holy Spirit within, then the decision must be made to break the barrier. God must be consulted about all things in our life, but so often we are waiting on Him to do the things that are within our power to execute. Again, we must keep in mind, while we make frequent, daily, and weekly decisions to postpone, cease, anticipate, pause and recess, father time does not wait, and God has not changed. His word still remains the same, but we have not made the real attempt to launch into the areas of really trusting Him. Growth will never take place in the comfort of our empire. We must relinquish all dominance to ourselves and become vulnerable to the faithfulness of God's promises to us all. The promise that we are never, ever alone is true. He hath said, "I will never leave thee, nor forsake thee" (Heb. 13:5) Pray in detail about your fears. Yes, that is what it is, fear. Apprehension, misgivings, dread, and uneasiness is all part of fear, yet we have not mentioned, the reaction of people, what they think, or what will be said, and the relationships that we will lose in the process. Nevertheless, a decision must be made because our life is forever affected by what we don't do, or someday later plan to do. Life on this earth is not forever, although we procrastinate as if it is. The statement "I wish I had," or "if I had it to do all over again," the point of the matter we have just one go of this life, so we must make it profitable. We have all said at one time or another, "I will do it later," but repetition will always cause us to make an appearance at our previous points of reference or, either in a recapitulated dialog. Keep in mind, it is always God's will for us to prosper and move in an onward direction. Let us all take a hard look at what we are saying and doing and pray for unfeigned recognition of our daily role. Pray for courage to make the necessary adjustments that align with His will for our lives. Keep in mind, that it is in Him (Christ Jesus) we live, move and have our being.

Focus

Chapter Four

Who has not struggled at some point in their life with keeping something as well defined as it should be? It happens to the best of us. When we think of focusing, our first thought is our eyesight and how well we can see what we are looking at. Rightfully so, anyone that can see, would want to have the most optimal vision that can be had. Premier vision is the goal at any age, even at an infant stage, a mother would want to know that her child has good eyesight. However, aside from the physical vision that most of us are blessed to have, there is another aspect of understanding the art of focusing. That is correct, it can become an art. The Merriam Webster dictionary states it well, that it's a skill acquired by experiences, study, or observation.

Why does it have to be a skill one might say? Because if the truth be told and honesty prevails, not many of us have mastered the ability to do anything without at one time or another, consenting to the interference, intrusion or suspension of a task. The ability to focus on the task at hand will require the study of ourselves and our vulnerability to being diverted. It will often require more than one failure to our approach before realizing that it is not easy as publicized. It is more than concentration, because that could be situational and momentary, however, most things that require focus are projects, intentions, and aspirations that have a purposeful and desired destination.

Real focus can result in a learning process about your strengths and weaknesses. People that are skillful in focusing are very productive, goal oriented, and can be prosperous in their accomplishments, because excuses are not their entertainment. The Bible references an eagle in several scriptures, because an eagle appears to fly high and remains focused on it's anticipated destination. The eagle's eyesight is keen and it pays very close attention to details.

Chapter Four: Focus

That could be a large downfall, is not paying attention to the everyday details in our life and before we realize, we are knee deep into a state of being what could have been nipped in the bud, meaning a swift destruction of something before it grows. It can be aborted before it is even dignified with a label.

Many adults would falsely assign themselves to having an Attention Deficit Hyperactivity Disorder (ADHD). While that is certainly a real disorder nevertheless, we have to be careful that it is not our self-imposed alibi, while choosing that label as a decoy. Learning our truths, about the person within will build fortitude in the undeviating system to our focus. Whatever maybe our focal point, the beginning strategy of maintaining that as the center of attention, is to ask ourselves, "how bad do you want it?" Which means, whatever is the focused purpose. There are all types of challenges in the process of focusing, from amazing to dreadful, nevertheless we must stay with it, having a sense of awareness, and the ability to be perceptive, while having an insight on our sensitivities to destructive devices that are part of living. Not everything that interrupts requires stoppage. The wisdom to know what to pause for, and the ability to keep it moving could be the determining factor to victory or defeat in any situation.

Many individuals abandon their intentions for the lack of knowing how to buffer the interruptions, knowing the course of action, and staying on the original inspired pathway.

Many people have their joy and enthusiasm sapped away due to the powerlessness they feel as a result of the frequent encountered visits to a repetitive landing place. It is often encouraging to have reference points to remind us that anything is possible regardless of the struggle. It is about getting beyond and through it, while understanding that help is on your side and that help is always provided by God himself. "So do not fear, for I am with you; do not be dismayed, for I am your God. I will strengthen you

Chapter Four: Focus

and help you; I will uphold you with my righteous right hand" (Isa.41:10). Everyone needs to know that there is a way through all things no matter what it is, and God is the way. Certainly, it is no failure to admit that being focused and staying focused in all phases of life can be a piece of work, but if we can remain vigilant with an eagle's eye, we will not miss the intended purpose.

Having the ability to see and envision the desired life objectives must be held close at the heart of man. Why? Because at the heart signifies being true to ourselves and we are more than likely to carry over the vision no matter what length of time it takes, rather than terminating it completely. Some struggle for years without the art of focusing on any particular thing, nevertheless, do not, ever give up the intended purpose nor allow any influence to rob and steal it. People will never stop being people, meaning human beings, mankind, humanity and flesh. What does that translate to mean?? FLAWED! However, we are created and empowered to

Chapter Four: Focus

overcome and win, so when things in life become intrusive and it will, ranging from anything to everything, pray to have a like focus of an eagle, meaning don't be moved until you reach it.

Move

Chapter Five

The ability to move is not to be still, but it brings to mind some form of activity. Even before knowing what it references to, it suggests some stimulating function to be occupied. Generally, people move when prompted in some particular way that validates the activity in motion, however, there are those that must be stimulated, urged, or motivated with an intended purpose to activate the pursuit. Certainly, there is nothing wrong with having an intended purpose to trigger the energetic impulse within. For some, doing, and activating the desire within does not require much. Some individuals live to execute the next task that presents itself. Nevertheless, you have those persons that require more than their own desire, because they fight their own battles within themselves that create barriers, which causes many of their desired tasks to be postponed. To crave without the fulfillment is like being driven to receive satisfaction, but walking away empty.

There is a time to be still and a time to move and get to the task we are purposed for. As humans, we conversate, chatter, plan, and debate regarding our ambitions and desires, however, we can become so occupied with the expressions of it all, we overlook that it is the action behind the verbalization that produces the desired outcome. Just as the Bible states that "Faith without works is dead" (James 2:26), it indicates the sophisticated manner in which we may communicate our goals and intentions, nevertheless, it is the application which we exert, that manifest the results and fulfillment of the desired outcome.

Believe it or not, making the effort, striving, and undertaking are a few of the many ingredients to the accomplishments to any task. God blesses what we do. Certainly, there is nothing wrong with declaring, and

Chapter Five: Move

affirming what we desire. That is a marvelous "kick-off" to the unfolding of something that can be great. However, the declaration of our purpose is not enough, and although it may produce enthusiasm, it is the execution that produces accomplishments. So, how is that achieved when there are so many obstacles that seem to complicate the efforts that are applied?

Well, it is the mindset, an established set of attitudes which begins the journey. The pattern of our thoughts affects the exhibit of our spirit. The power of our mindset is everything, because without it, there is no strength behind our deeds. Everything that we do begins with the gesture of the mind. We have the power within ourselves to forgo it, or begin the process of maneuvering it into something that could become everything. No one starts in the middle of something, but there is a beginning point, a time to launch whatever is to be possessed. We must be careful to not just become stimulated by the discussion of

Chapter Five: Move

our motivations. It is a space that we can linger too long, which can transition into a posture that is not so easy to surrender. Praying for the right mindset is profitable. The Bible states "be ye transformed by the renewing of your mind, that ye may prove what is that good, and acceptable, and perfect, will of God" (Romans 12:2). The renewal of our mind must take place every day. Just as we bathe daily and more often within a day depending on the task at hand, because to feel clean and fresh provides a revitalization and restoration to the next function at hand. This is the same concept for a mind renewal. It is important to have a resuscitated mind, meaning to breathe new life into our thoughts daily. It precipitates a new outlook for each day, which prompts the performance of our destiny.

The performance of our purpose is personal. It is one of those positions in this journey that we must forgo solo, meaning each individual must decide what life will look like for themselves. However, HIGH

Chapter Five: Move

ALERT! Sometimes we have one plan, but God has another plan for our lives. Nevertheless, it is our submissiveness to His plan that makes the journey rewarding. Is it a smooth and easy pathway? Absolutely not, nevertheless, the bumps in the road is not a showstopper, yet it becomes intentional to meet the objective goal. Yes, challenges along this expedition are part of the travel package. Without them, maturation, achievement, and ratification cannot be attained. Therefore, we must expect some oppositions, and cannot allow fear to cancel the movement of our endeavors. Why? Because this is personal, and we must answer to God and confront ourselves if we abandon the purpose. The initiation begins the process, yes, it is a process, but that is okay, besides, making a cake is a process, nevertheless, we are willing to see it through, because we want the completed product.

So, how does one repudiate what has never been carried out? Oftentimes we predict the

Chapter Five: Move

outcome of something unfamiliar without the introduction of the reveal. Movement into something new will take courage and confidence. Both are essential to the success of the endeavor. Without a change in mental, emotional and physical practices, transformation cannot be perpetrated. The goal of moving, is to evade the tradition of repetitive dialog that yields no fruit by itself. We are all looking, and in pursuit of the optimal outcome in our lives. However, what we often bypass is the sacrifice and labor that it cost to harvest the benefits. The only benefit that is known to humans, without a cost, which provides everlasting life, is the penalty paid by Jesus Christ himself for all mankind. The Bible states "For you were bought at a price; therefore, glorify God in your body and in your spirit, which are God's" (1Corthin 6:20).

In addition, the Bible states " For what I received I passed on to you as of first importance that Christ died for our sins according to the Scriptures, that he was

Chapter Five: Move

buried, that he was raised on the third day according to the Scriptures" (1Corthin 15:3-4 NIV). We the people are free to live and be prosperous in the process. Therefore, we must change our position and do not be afraid to proceed forward. Pray about everything, and as the peace of God permeates our spirit, monitor how God modifies, converts and administrates the course of our pathway.

Pick Up the Pace

Chapter Six

The thought of increasing the pace brings to mind a rate or speed of something. The only reason anyone would have a need to move a little quicker is if they were knowingly moving too slow to accomplish the necessary need at hand. We all have a starting point to everything we set out to accomplish or perform, nevertheless oftentimes we become complacent with the effort of our intended approach. Comfortability can sometimes be a confidant, too closely connected. In order to enhance the course of this journey, it mandates aborting the leisurely way of proceeding, and conclude, that in order to create an effective way of achieving, we must draw in our minds for production. Life is not about only making something of ourselves, but being an effective contributor in the life of someone else. Whatever is meant to be achieved from our pathway, it may necessitate an acceleration of movement on our part to make it happen.

We all are well aware that life here on this earth is not forever, and although we may not run to do everything, nevertheless, the abuse we absorb by our laggard information, may yield a great deal of unfruitful time that cannot be retrieved. The Bible states "See then that you walk circumspectly, not as fools but as wise, redeeming the time, because the days are evil. Therefore, do not be unwise, but understand what the will of the Lord is" (Eph.5: 15-17). Redeeming the time can mean recovering our time from waste to improve it for greater purposes. It is understood that to make decisions in haste is not always a good idea. It is also wise to think before acting and pray about new tasks to be taken. However, once those very important steps have been achieved and there is an assurance and peace to move ahead, then we must spring forward like there is an agenda to be reckoned with.

Chapter Six: Pick Up the Pace

It will all start with a heart that craves to fulfill life's purpose. The question may be, why must it begin with cravings? Because when you crave for something, an urge within is triggered and will not be content until the appetite for it is satisfied. In addition, the powerful desire to fulfill that appetite prompts an individual to hasten the activity toward the intended purpose. Taking steps toward the increasing of momentum will produce great dividends. There are some instances when time is everything in regard to reaping the harvest at an appointed time. Some things are presented only once in a lifetime, and if the opportunity is missed, it may not come around in the same package. Therefore, it is vital for us to be vigilant to ourselves and the latitude that engages our space. We must pray for a spirit of recognition, to be able to identify the designs of life that cross our pathways, acknowledge that the only hindrance is ourselves, and concede that we do nothing alone but all things are done with the help of God. Whether we realize it or not, fear

Chapter Six: Pick Up the Pace

presents itself in many colors, sizes, and shapes, therefore, if we do not understand it that way, we could be stagnant, and drowning in the spirit of our bodies. Lacking courage and confidence could be the challenger of our tempo. Lacking the bravery and validity toward the approach of our purpose being "full speed ahead" will delay, and enhance stagnation in unwanted places of our lives.

We may wonder why there is that certain pivotal area we cannot get beyond? However, don't be dismayed, because it is always 100% God's will for us to soar above all interferences. Unproductive time in our life benefits no one and adds to our dialog of, "if I only had, or "wish I could do it all over again" list. Picking up the pace, for achievement, puts the responsibility on ourselves. Yes, that is what we don't want, is the responsibility of our own deficiencies because it holds us accountable, and it is always less burdensome to make it someone else's defect, then we are relieved of the weight regarding the absence of our own progression. Picking up the pace means we must be present, in our mind, and our thinking, which satisfies being true to ourselves and to our God. That truth permeates our spirit and produces the surrendering of what pleases God and that is to fulfill His purpose. When a person picks up the pace of walking or running, they obviously reach their destination much faster than one whom strolls the same pathway, deviating with every distraction. However, when a person moves at a steady, consistent rate of movement, there is a concentration and focus that must accompany that role.

Most of the time when there is a consistency, it means there is an agenda that must be met and no distraction has enough worth to diverge from the focal point. There is a quote that states a bull dog's faith is aggressive, he bites down and won't let go. There is a motivation we can take from this quote. The era of time that we live in today, we must take the aggressive approach to accomplish the desired goals. We must pray

Chapter Six: Pick Up the Pace

for a strong mind and a rhythm to our move. So, what is meant by rhythm? A pace and flow that is consistent, unwavering, determined, and supported with a craving that will linger until the appetite is satisfied.

Plan to Win

Chapter Seven

For some individuals, planning comes easy and it is their way of life. Everything they do or set forth to do is thought through and planned for. However, there are those individuals that plan for very little and believe in living on the edge or spontaneously in almost all things they do. Well, as in anything, there can be something negative and positive to both depending on the way it is viewed. The benefit of planning anything is to gain ambition and have a strategy toward the desired outcome. Planning provides us with a plot through the passage to our designated purpose. Could the same desire be accomplished without a plan? Not saying that it could not, however, the probability of being diverted with interferences, intrusions, and other interests will be the height of the climb. There are many things each day, month, and year that

Chapter Seven: Plan to Win

exist to entice us all from the center of our attention, nevertheless, it is the strength of our will, and the expression of it, through our actions, that determines the execution of the master plan. Yes, planning is intentional, purposeful, and deliberately put through the process of thought, consideration, and premeditated aspirations to target the end product.

We plan to do many things such as travel, further our education, marry, have children, increase our income, relocate our lives to other localities, and the list goes on, therefore, good, bad, or indifferent, it is an agenda put in motion with an anticipated desire to be reached. The question to be proposed and answered is, do we have enough tenacity and backbone to work it out and WIN?? We proclaim that we do, however, to live the process of the stratagem, succumbs to its own classification. Winning is that word we all love to hear, from the time we are children, because it does not feel good to lose and winning leaves a smile on our faces, no

Chapter Seven: Plan to Win

matter who we are. Nevertheless, most individuals that win in any area of life, have done so, as a result of having an objective and a masterplan. That's correct, a master plan in place sets the agenda for getting it done. It all begins with a passion for what we are moving toward, and a devotion with commitment not to quit until it happens. Since winning is the desired goal, be prepared for those challenges that will be part of the journey, however, fear not, and don't allow it to be a deterrent because it is just temporary if there is a true commitment. Feet planting is essential when planning to win. What is meant by this, is being steadfast and unworried about the various disturbances that become a part of the process, because if it's not expected, then it could blindside a person and give rise to discouragement which will only trigger an urge to abandon it all.

What joy it is to feel the triumph of succeeding in something that we have travailed, worked hard, and sacrificed for in some fashion. Even when the sacrifice is

Chapter Seven: Plan to Win

part of the waiting process. Yes, waiting can be tough, although we have the Bible that supports waiting, it states; They that wait upon the LORD shall renew their strength; they shall mount up with wings as eagles; they shall run, and not be weary; and they shall walk, and not faint (Isa. 40:31 KJV). In order to have the tenacity to wait, there must first be a desire that accompanies a vision for the expected win. Yes, expected, because if there is not an expectation for the desired victory, then the battle was lost at the start. The anticipation, without anxiety, activates the excitement of what is yet to come. There has to be a mindset to win and making it a "must have," according to the will of the Lord, makes it official. Making plans to win means becoming organized in our thoughts and understanding, that although the pathway may not be without hiccups, nevertheless, it cannot be a deal breaker of the focal point. There must be an expectation of oppositions, if not, the readiness to manage the win may be in question. Preparation for winning also

Chapter Seven: Plan to Win

signifies that we are making provisions to be a recipient of vision.

Individuals that think it makes a person that plans, too rigid, is usually a person that is not well-organized and feels what they desire, will work out somehow. Yes, it is that somehow, that leads the way for calamity to enter the arena. Part of the plan to win requires the positivity of dialog. There is no room for negativity, because it will only become a stumbling block. Positive thinking, speaking, and fellowships will maintain the momentum of the atmosphere. It is important to keep the climate of our daily customs consistent. Praying for a daily mind renewal is a must. Without a fresh mind each day, it limits and prevents the ability to receive the introduction of new discoveries. Stagnation will merge in and become the barrier that can become a difficult task to move. We cannot afford to allow defeatism to enter the process of this great launch to win, therefore, regardless of what someone may suggest, if it does not align with the concept

Chapter Seven: Plan to Win

of what it takes to be a winner, then, they are speaking another language. We must make the necessary adjustments, and posture ourselves for the win God predestined us to have.

Mine Your Own Business

Chapter Eight

When we say "mine," we inevitably are speaking of ourselves and what pertains to us as an individual. My affairs are my business, responsibility, and domain. There was an old song with words that stated, "you got 6 months to mind your own business, and 6 months to leave mine alone." Now that was not a threat, but a point of matter. As we know, the sum of those two numbers equals a total of twelve months, which is 365 days, better known as one full year. It is believed that the interpretation translates to mean, it takes every day of our lives to attend to ourselves individually. Humanity has made it habitual to find the affairs of others more consuming than themselves, to the point that the spot light seems to pivot in the direction of others and we have faded

Chapter Eight: Mine Your Own Business

out of the forefront of our own point of interest. If there was an honest evaluation of me, myself, and I, it would be discovered that it is a full-time employment that provides no time for annual leave. Most adults and even the very young can be very complex human beings that take a lifetime to maintain self-awareness.

Maybe taking notes of who we really are becomes too complex to decipher. However, it often seems when analyzing someone else, the knowledge of who they are and what they should do flows like a surge of endless waters. Why do we have, or think we have the answers for the lives of others? Why do we see, or think we see, their lives so crystal clear? Why do we seem to know or think we know them far better, then they know themselves????? How is it that, if they would just do it our way, their life would soar above the sky???? If true honesty would prevail, that is what a large percentage of humanity experiences during a lifetime. It is an important element in our journey that we must become aware of,

Chapter Eight: Mine Your Own Business

because if we evade it, we will cripple our own personal growth. The objective of this awareness is to terminate this practice and become the nucleus of our own lives.

We are all powerful human beings that fall short of recognizing the measure of influence we sustain because the inspections are not a consistent self-examination, but a scrutinization and inspection of our neighbor. Once we begin the training process of investigating our strengths and vulnerabilities, then we can begin to birth our true identity, and what we can be to the human race abroad. Whenever we make a commitment to improve our lives and move into the broad scope of living our purpose, the true advancement transpires when we serve a summons upon ourselves first. Creating a summons for ourselves requires taking some uncomfortable evaluations of who we are within and allowing TRUTH to be our indictment.

Truth begins with our thought process, and determining if the process is producing growth, or resulting in pointless repetition. CAUTION, in many ways, our life can very well exhibit the product of our thinking. Yes, a hard truth, but there it emerges. The Bible states "For as he thinks in his heart, so *is* he" (Proverbs 23: 7 NLJV). From the mind and heart, it emanates through our spirit. It will be who we are, unless there is a recognition of a necessity to transform. Transformation is a time-consuming process that requires modification and alterations. Adjustments that are vital to reshaping and adaptation that we cannot fear. To undertake a self-project such as this, leaves no time to busybody into the experience of another. Praying for individuals is one matter that we perform but are supposed to abandon at the altar. If what we pray for is not discarded into God's hands, then we are in a lane we do not belong, and precious time is being exhausted, in a space that could be transfigured into a better identity of ourselves.

The hard truth is, if our precious time was engrossed on fixing our deficiencies,

Chapter Eight: Mine Your Own Business

tweaking and refining the God given gifts and potential awarded to us, we could hear the voice of the Lord directing and engineering the stronger and preferred human he created. Conversation, chatter, and points of views do not change anyone or any situation, however, PRAYER, concentration, and application into our role in time, will bestow the reformation we crave. We must be careful that our life practices are not being spent on shallow performances, meaning time consuming labor, with no depth and yields no progress. Time is our present, and it is one of the most precious gifts given to us to be exercised for the furtherance of reaching the destiny of purpose for our lives, and the more we use it, to refine the inward spirit of ourselves, there will be no time available to engage in the space of another. Our self-rehabilitation will give the world our best time and will leave the orchestration of others where it belongs, in the mighty hands of God.

Pay Attention

Chapter Nine

Having a sense of awareness in life and our daily environment, can make all the difference in our world. Too often people are going about each day with a preoccupation, only of their current task, with no consciousness of others, the condition of the world, nor the community in which they emerge. There cannot be any biases about being cognizant of others. Our living and serving in this world is most profitable when we are inclined to the needs of our neighbors. Oftentimes there are situations occurring in our immediate habitat, without a noteworthy response, all because there is a preoccupation of something further from our direct surroundings. Unintentionally, we miss the most important things that require awareness, or acknowledgement due to careless oversights that many times have

Chapter Nine: Pay Attention

resulted from the lack of being able to prioritize the principle objectives in our personal domain.

It is humanistic, to make mistakes, as no one dots every I, and crosses every T in the process of living, nevertheless, the desire to identify the necessities as they present, should be the preference of human nature.

Who hasn't occasionally noted there was an oversight, for something very important due to some form of distraction that engrossed their attentiveness momentarily? It has happened to the best of us however, it should be our goal to minimize the frequency of those manifestations. Paying close attention first to ourselves, and then to the community in which we live and serve is paramount. Staying alert to life, can make all the difference in our current state of living, and the futuristic goals we cherish. The Bible tells us …Be alert and of sober mind. Your enemy the devil prowls around like a roaring lion looking for someone to devour (1Pet. 5:8 NIV). That means we are not exempt

Chapter Nine: Pay Attention

from personal attacks that test our fortitude in God daily, monthly, yearly or at any given time. Our life must be planted upon a foundation, that is solid and anchored in the reliability and promises of God Himself.

There are times, when God is trying to show us something through various situations and circumstances, however, without careful attentiveness to our daily role as people created by God, and the purpose we have on this earth, we can so easily miss what is very apparent before our eyes. Because life happens to us all, we must pray for help and strength to stay alert to our experiences, so that we do not miss the specific part that will provoke us into our destiny. Becoming vigilant, kindles movement when necessary, and to pause when warranted. There is no better feeling than to be in time for an anticipated event and knowing that all have been captured, however, there is such disappointment, when the expiration has occurred due to a pattern of neglect, dominated by the process. There is a reason why being fully awake is the preferred state of survival. The opportunity to nip in the bud, the misleading, and power it down with prayer, in addition to the word of God, will more than likely manifest the intended triumph, our faith delivers. Vigilance awards us the opportunity, to dodge unwanted imbalances, and win the more profitable outcomes.

As believers in Christ Jesus, we must keep in mind, it is perpetually God's will and plan for us to live our best life while we soar into thriving effectively, and arriving at the peak of our purpose. Never think any of this is accomplished alone. Understand what the will of the Lord is and the scripture that says

.. For in him we live, and move, and have our being; as certain also of your own poets have said, for we are also, his offspring (Acts 17:28 KJV). We must establish a daily prayer to remain vigilant, and the distractions will less likely obstruct our assignment. Being observant awards us the sensitivity to the spirit and feelings of others. It sharpens our sense of perception, and births a discernment, which leads to a

Chapter Nine: Pay Attention

broader scope of percipience. We cannot afford to catnap through our journey, because it diminishes the clarity needed to comprehend what the will of the Lord is and the path He navigates. Remember to pray for vigilance, it will reduce the bumps in the road and lead to the fulfillment of our purpose.

Don't Judge the View

Chapter Ten

It is human nature to establish an opinion about something based on its appearances, however, is it the right thing to do? Probably not, because many things in this world are not as they appear, nevertheless, it is part of humanity to deem it to be one way or the other, based on its disguise. These assumptions, can potentially, obstruct our ability to discern what could ultimately, be the factor of reward. As individuals, we live with desires, needs, goals, and visions regardless of what they may be, however, it is imperative, that we avoid the habitual need to draw conclusions on natural eyesight only. Who hasn't at one time or another, mistakenly thought they saw one thing, but it consequently resulted in something completely different? We make efforts in our lives to accomplish particular tasks, or goals that oftentimes appear to be headed in the opposite direction. Not to mention the

Chapter Ten: Don't Judge the View

frequent prayers we offer unto the Lord, that we consider ourselves to be namely, patiently waiting for, however, when there is not a soon to be notable answer, our spirit becomes affected by what we do not physically see with the natural eyesight.

We must remember our prayers are based on FAITH, which is the substance of things hoped for, the evidence of things not seen (Heb 11:1 KJV). We unintentionally imprison ourselves, meaning lock away our advancement, because our eyesight has been clouded by what we physically see rather than what we, by faith believe. It takes great tenacity, character, and consistency to grasp faith without wavering, when the desired objective is not in view. The unseen, is so often, a deep seeded supplication, that affects the inward spirit, which we employ in our lives daily, as we interact with mankind. The measure of our influence, we may never know, therefore, it is imperative that our spirit is preserved to effectively be productive in the lives of those we connect with from day to day. Therefore, we must

Chapter Ten: Don't Judge the View

remain mindful, not to form an opinion, or draw conclusions from our human feelings or observations, because the judgment of our view is more than likely, not accurate of the spiritual reality. With that in mind, our faith will remain strong and our spirit elevated. The Bible quotes..Finally my brethren, be strong in the Lord and in the power of His might..(Eph. 6:10 KJV). We are not alone in this appointment of life. The Bible also states.. Surely God is my help; the Lord is the one who sustains me (Psalms 54:4 NIV). Therefore, when our humanistic acuity begins to dominate our visual effects, we must pray for strength that our judgment will not transcend what we spiritually know. We must accept nothing less than to triumph over the elements that contribute to the vague appearance of what we see and shun drawing a premature conclusion on the promise expected. Visuality is a powerful tool when used wisely, prayerfully and with purpose.

Fight

Chapter Eleven

Ordinarily, the first thought that comes to mind when using the word "fight" is combative or aggressive, however, there are other ways to use the word in a different context, wherein fighting can be a component that can produce favorable outcomes. When we are young, most are taught not to fight or avoid situations that would result in some sort of physical altercation, because the consequences would possibly result in someone being physically hurt or wounded. Therefore, to steer clear of that type of aftermath, fighting should always be evaded. However, there's always more than one way of understanding how an element works.

Let's think of a non-physical way of fighting. Yes, that is what it will take sometimes, to make it, survive, or be

Chapter Eleven: Fight

successful. Winning is the result of fighting without quitting, however, the undertaking of this type of engagement will require a mental, and emotional commitment with a broad mindset that generates a spirit to fight. To fight means having the will, mental strength, and emotional endurance to persevere, from beginning to end. The onset of any situation is usually hopeful and promising until hope is put through the test of time, meaning days, weeks, months and yes, even years. When time becomes the focal point, then the element of a non-physical fight begins.

The test of what our mental and emotional state can withstand, and what will be the endorsement that will provide support, until the conclusion of the whole matter, is the theme. When the warfare of prayer fills the atmosphere, and there is no sign of victory, how do we re-posture our human nature from its response, to what we would naturally feel? Yes, it can be very testy. But there is a way out and a way of escape. If there is one small mustard seed of faith, that can be manufactured, in the loins of our soul and spirit, then, that shall be the foundation of our lifeline.

Remember the Bible verse... and having done all to stand, stand therefore (Eph. 6:13-14). Just to seize that captivating part of the verse is the essence of the kind of instruction that must become the dialog of our thoughts. The bible states .. Thou wilt keep him in perfect peace, whose mind is stayed on thee: because he trusteth in thee (Isa. 26:3). Yes, TRUST, is a very big word during the test of times, nevertheless, most of the conductivity of our life is based on trust even without thinking about it. We trust the chair we sit in, the air we breathe, the water we drink and the list goes on, so why not trust the creator of all mankind? The LORD *is* on my side; I will not fear. What can man do to me (Ps. 118:6 NKJV)?

Check out some successful keys to fight:

1. Pray for a fresh mindset daily.
2. Monitor what you say. Un-effective words are lethal.

Chapter Eleven: Fight

3. Don't get hung up on who is right or wrong.
4. Pray for a broader scope of seeing things.
5. Pray for continuity of consistency. Being inconsistent creates stagnation.
6. Pray daily about the distractions, because they will exist.
7. Don't abort your vision.
8. No matter what, keep it moving.
9. Don't allow a lack of humility become your downfall.
10. Pray for joy. Remember, the joy of the Lord is your strength.
11. Pray for direction and guidance. At times, you won't know which way to turn.
12. Crave to win. Don't stop until you do.

Health Weights

Chapter Twelve

It may be difficult to accept that our health could possibly be a weight within itself, however, it can unconsciously become such, without realizing it. If health is a state of being free from sickness and disease, then why does it so often become the warfare of our minds? For those that are born in this world with certain afflictions beyond control we have not sufficient answers, however, those that are born and considered to be healthy individuals must seek to comprehend the cause, as why living to have good health becomes a weighted factor in our lives. Along the journey of life, beginning at birth, vaccines are administered to keep us free from diseases, nevertheless, throughout each stage of life, mild to complex, illnesses are acquired to aid in the building of our immunity. Since, we have the will and option to nutritionally consume our desired appetite, the return we receive, in the mastery of our health often, determines the quality of our life. When the characteristics of our health begin to stipulate the value of our everyday activity, there must be an awakening to what, why, and how. What are we doing that affects our health? Why do we choose to manage ourselves the way we do? And how do we employ our daily practices? These may considerably be uncomfortable questions to answer, however, let the truth have a voice.

When convictions of this nature begin to circulate our thoughts, this is a hunch, that corrections are the prospect of the future. At this point, we can choose a course of action or resort to a way out of the inevitable. If not careful, the status of our wellbeing can become a situation that becomes a responsibility unavoidable. A plight that can be weighted and difficult to supervise, will be the frontline of our everyday occupation, and included in the choosing of our recreation. Our health should be enjoyed to support life, a gift granted to us by the grace of God, but when we abandon the critical necessity to pay attention at all times, to the home which buttresses our soul, then the evidence will speak loud and clear. Our health does not have to be heavy, in the respect of unmanageable, it just requires attention, in the part of our spirit, called love. Loving ourselves enough to give it the best we have, without leaving it in arms way. No need to shorten our time here on earth when we have so much to do.

God needs every available hand to serve in His kingdom and be a drawing agent to show someone the way, to the life he so freely has given to all mankind. We all have been awarded gifts and abilities from God to be shared with the whole world and no one has been left out of being a recipient. We must have or develop a sense of awareness to the elements that trigger the things we must evade. Our ability to promote as individuals could be stagnant, without the tools within ourselves to overshadow the fluctuations that spin our way. There are enough weights in living that will challenge the trip of life, therefore we must take authority over the territory that we have the power to conquer. So, when our health becomes the focal point of our struggle, waste no time, but institute prayer immediately. The Bible instructs us to ..Pray without ceasing (1Thess. 5:17). In addition, the Bible states that ...The effectual fervent prayer of a righteous man availeth much (James 5:16). We can win over the battle of our Health disparities.

It tends to be an area of our lives, that the adversary plots to steal and rob from us all, if we will permit it. However, we have the power to nip it in the bud when the challenges present. Here are just a few daily tips you should do, to enhance your health status:

1. Pay attention to how you feel each day.
2. Monitor the way all classifications of foods leave you feeling after ingesting them.

Chapter Twelve: Health Weights

3. Be willing to make the necessary adjustments, it will become the lifestyle you must accept.

4. Never compare your health needs to someone else, your fine-tuning is customized for you.

5. Pray for strength to be discipline and consistent in your endeavors, you will always need the help of God.

Live

Chapter Thirteen

Oftentimes people personalize how they define living and what it means. Consequently, it has a diverse meaning to a large scope of individuals. For some, the description of living is limited, and to others it may be extensive. The outlook on living can depend upon an individual's perception of their own life and the success or failure of it. There are people that exist, meaning they are breathing in some form, whether it is normal or abnormal, and the blood in their body continues to circulate naturally or mechanically. However, the Bible tells us that.... The thief cometh not, but for to steal, and to kill, and to destroy; I am come that they might have life, and that they might have it more abundantly (John 10:10 KJV). Jesus here is speaking about any man. He came to earth and sacrificed His life that mankind would receive life and obtain life

Chapter Thirteen: Live

overflowing. The pending question is, do we want to live? and how do we want to live our life? It can only be answered by each individual person.

Believe it or not, we do have choices, and the option of how we desire to live the life given to us, is certainly an independent decision. All too frequent, we tend to accuse others or our circumstances, for the quality of life we have or do not have, but then, ultimately, we have the responsibility to make every effort to build the life we desire and hope for. Living and creating the type of life preferred, often requires a lot of courage, because everyone does not have the same beginning that awards them, what appears to be an easier route by way of association. Nevertheless, in spite of the rough beginning in life, we are expected to find a way to pull through and survive. Yes, survive, meaning persist, continue, hold on, abide, linger, and get through. There is no affordability awarded by mankind to make excuses for the disparities of life's experiences. Sometimes, it almost seems

Chapter Thirteen: Live

there is an expectation to do a reversal, in the mist of any and all of life's hurdles. Well, it can be done, but not alone. We become vulnerable when help is needed, however, that is where we are when life happens.

Vulnerability is exactly where the Lord wants us to be, in need of care and protection from Him. The Bible states…So we may boldly say: "The LORD *is* my helper;
I will not fear. What can man do to me? (Heb. 13:16) The Bible also states…Surely God is my help the Lord is the one who sustains me (Ps: 54:4 NIV). Our dependency upon Him provides us with the assurance that the Lord will meet us right where we are, and allow us the affordability to live. So, what does LIVE really mean? Well, we could say it means something different to each person and we would not be wrong, however, to really live is to first, know God the creator, learn him for yourself, choose to grow in the relationship, as in any other

Chapter Thirteen: Live

connection, where there is a deep desire to feel close. From the commitment formed through the relationship with God, will evolve, joy, peace, contentment, and confidence of who we are. More than anything, The Lord Jesus wants us all to be happy and at peace. The Bible states... and the peace of God, which surpasses all understanding, will guard your hearts and minds through Christ Jesus (Phil. 4:7). Living our best life means to be at peace with ourselves, decline negativity of any kind, know who we are for sure, and avoid bending to the obstacles that intersect our path. We must always reach for the best, regardless of what it looks like, because things will not always look the part, of what we are reaching for, nevertheless, go for it anyway. We must not be so quick to give up, but fight for what we want and need. As the late Representative Elijah Cummings often recited, a poem by Parren J. Mitchell, I only have a minute, sixty seconds is in it, force upon me I did not choose it, but I know that I must use it, I suffer if I lose it,

Chapter Thirteen: Live

give an account if I abuse it, only a tiny little minute but eternity is in it. LIVE.

Gratitude

Chapter Fourteen

The ability to be thankful is believed to come natural for most individuals, however, not necessarily true. It is assumed to be one of those very common words that would naturally roll out of our mouth at the appropriate time to be spoken, but without the foundation being laid for the use of this common phrase "Thank you" it will not automatically become the expression of choice, at the time most expected to be articulated. When a person thinks of having gratitude, the automatic thought to mind is thankfulness, and appreciation for something or everything. However, can you imagine that formulating this expression can often be a challenging factor when the times in our life do not measure an appreciation for the discovery it exhibits?

Nevertheless, there is a way of learning how to be thankful regardless of the experiences

Chapter Fourteen: Gratitude

dealt to us. Is it an effort? Yes. Is it easy? Not always. But it is absolutely fruitful and profitable. It seems to be habitual, of automatically thinking and speaking of the undesirable, unlikable things in our lives, meanwhile, the blessings to be counted, are an after-thought to be reckoned with. It seems to take mind power to calculate the countless components of blessings we daily possess, especially when life begins to test the affirmation in which we live by.

In the meantime, there is an internal awareness, that it is someone else much worse than ourselves, and if we would just pause, and start our gratitude recognizing, that we are blessed to breathe, which identifies us to be living human beings, than that potentially can lead to the rise of investments into ourselves, paying great dividends. The bible states give thanks in all circumstances; for this is God's will for you in Christ Jesus (1Thess. 5:18 NIV) The practice of having gratitude provides us with a different mindset of how we view things in general. Yes, practice, which activates the

Chapter Fourteen: Gratitude

application of a method to behave by. We cannot condemn, something we have not tried. Start the rehearsal of being thankful by thinking it first, therefore, developing a mindset for it, will create a spirit within to feel the gratitude and develop the words of thankfulness, from out of your mouth.

The declaration of saying "thank you" can be a life changer. There is always a situation or set of circumstances, which can become a vocal piece of whining, and achieves absolutely no advancement in life, meanwhile, creates an abundance of discontent, frustration, and infirmities. Now, who would the gratitude be directed to first and foremost? None other than our creator, Jesus Christ himself, who has given us life and the ability to make choices. Yes, being part of the human race permits us to have options, and a will to make decisions, good or bad. Gratitude for all things in life, wakes up the acknowledgement, and appreciation for details in our life that we do not automatically perceive as blessings and possibly take for granted. Yes, it is not easy

Chapter Fourteen: Gratitude

to admit, that there are things or people we do not value, and cherish, or should it be stated that "we do in our heart or intentions," but never reveal it to be so. It becomes a careless operation of administration with values, and lacking the thought process, of what it takes to sustain its viability.

Therefore, to maintain a heart and mindset of gratitude, just may take more effort than we anticipate. Remember, it is our normal human nature that becomes our battle ground to overcome and gain victory over.

Here are a few helpful points to maintain a spirit of gratitude:

1. Pray for a grateful heart and mind. Our method of thinking is everything.

2. Avoid the habit of complaining. It produces a spirit of discouragement.

3. Start your day by thanking God for life. It leads the way for gratitude.

Chapter Fourteen: Gratitude

4. Don't take adversities personally. There's always someone worse off than you.

5. Take the time to name what you do have, and start with yourself. Surprise!

6. Pray for consistency being grateful. It yields a life of abundance.

7. Make an attempt to list your blessings. It will change your perspective.

8. Speak positively, regardless of what you feel. Watch your dialog change.

9. Don't entertain the disappointments. It shortens the visit with you.

10. Don't be defined by your situations. A grateful spirit will always display the best of you.

The Best of You

Chapter Fifteen

There is good in all humanity, although we often wonder about the truth of that statement. The factualness of all individuals being good or having the ability to be good is a matter of fact, based on the confirming elements presented. The Bible states... God saw all that He had made, and it was very good (Gen. 1:31 NIV). It is imperative to understand that God makes no junk, and all creation is valued for its purpose. We are blessed to be made in the image of God. The Bible states.. So God created man in His own image, in the image of God created He him; male and female created He them (Gen.1:27 KJV). Therefore, we are fortunate to be part of humanity and in the likeness of the almighty God. During the course of living, there are situations that create a space

Chapter Fifteen: The Best of You

of vulnerability in our life, and often forms a scene of misrepresentation of what things really are. Without vigilance, our self-esteem is affected, and the beauty that complements the person we are.

No two individuals are exactly alike, and that is the beauty in who we are. Although, there are individuals we admire, however, to be unique is priceless. Everyone of us is born with gifts and potentials to be shared throughout the world, beginning with our immediate environment. Circumstances have a tendency to camouflage our sense of awareness and conceal our appeal to the world. Nevertheless, it is high time we become the drivers behind the wheel of the vehicle call life. God controls the directions because He navigates for us, however, we have the power within us, to press the gas pedal and move forward.

Yes, forward by first recognizing our internal beauty, for that is what God see's when He looks at us all. We are not defined by the opinion of others, because if their opinion is permitted to souse our mind, then we will never absorb the elements of growth. That's right, growth, the development of our advancement and the component that produces the greater part of our life. It is God's will for us all to learn from our experiences, grow in grace, and prosper in the walkway of life. There must be a stoppage in the act of reducing ourselves, as it deteriorates the beauty naturally possessed. Internally we pray, around the clock, and disclose the intentions of the heart, looking for God to release the beautiful elements of His gifts that were granted to us at conception, but robbed by the warfare of life. It is time to shine in the light of God's presence and stop hiding behind the shadow of defeat, because we are the beauty of God's creation and nothing can change it.

"You"

You must identify who you are, and begin to list the positive things you possess. There must be a conscious effort on your part to

Chapter Fifteen: The Best of You

daily confirm the positivity of who you are internally first, as it maneuvers through your spirit illuminating humanity, by your daily presence. You are one of a kind, whether acknowledged or not, is an unmatched feature by itself. It is for you, to be thrilled to look different and have qualities that are like no other person upon the earth. Yes qualities, the features, trademarks, and characteristics, that identifies you for being the person you are. You should no longer allow the establishments of this life to determine, and dictate, the distinctiveness for which artistry you possess, awarded to you by God our creator. The Bible states…It is He that has made us and not we ourselves (Ps.100:3). Therefore, you must begin to secure the honor upon yourself, to feel the privilege to have been, not only created by our heavenly father, but to be so uniquely formed.

Now let's examine your gifts. Yes, you possess gifts whether you acknowledge them to be so, or not. Your abilities, flair, touch, technique, aptitude, knack, and the list, goes on. If the chatter you hear says otherwise, then it is negativity that you must abort immediately, and not become a guest for its entertainment. Terminate negativity from your life, it can only impair your spirit and diminish the skillfulness of your craft. Nevertheless, if you find that is happening, or has occurred in your life, there is a way of escape and you hold the key.

Note these important key factors:

- Start your day with a prayer. It makes a huge difference in your launch.

- Steer clear, of the things you disfavor about yourself.

- Speak positive words internally and your exterior will possess it.

- Don't participate in negative dialog, it yields no fruit for you.

- Pray the Lord helps you to see yourself the way He does, it's a transformation.

- Pray for wisdom. It's priceless.

Chapter Fifteen: The Best of You

- Note your good qualities, and wear them. Your outfit will be one of a kind.

- Understand, it will be a process to be confident in your own shoes. Keep walking, you will step into your purpose.

- Hold your head up at all times, it will give you posture.

- You have what it takes to make it, that is your declaration.

Weights

Ex. Procrastination
_____

People
_____

_____

_____

_____

_____

_____

_____

_____

Spiritual Goals

Your Visions

Notes

www.ingramcontent.com/pod-product-compliance
Lightning Source LLC
Chambersburg PA
CBHW061453040426
42450CB00007B/1336